Think It Not Strange

Strange

Making Peace With Chronic Pain

Claudette Palatsky

Xulon
PRESS

Think It Not Strange
by Claudette Palatsky

Edited by B. Kay Coulter

Printed in the United States of America

Library of Congress Control Number: 2003103082
ISBN 1-591605-49-0

Unless otherwise indicated, all Bible quotations are taken from the New King James Version of the Bible. Copyright © 1979, 1980, 1982 by Thomas Nelson, Inc. (Bold and underlined emphasis are the author's and only for the purpose of highlighting relevant points in the context.)

Xulon Press
www.xulonpress.com

To order additional copies,
call 1-866-909-BOOK (2665).

Contents

Introduction

∽

> "Beloved, do not think it strange concerning
> the fiery trial which is to try you, as though
> some strange thing happened to you."
> (1 Peter 4:12)

As the Bible verse above illustrates, pain is a fiery trial. In this furnace of affliction the heat is certainly turned up and the smothering smoke of suffering becomes thick and threatening. The torment is real. It is personal. It disrupts lives, interrupts plans, and dealing with it day in and day out can appear to suck the life out of a person. Seemingly unanswered prayers for healing leave behind a trail of suffering. These afflicted individuals include the dissatisfied, disappointed, disillusioned, and the disheartened. But it does not always have to be that way! When the bottom drops out from beneath us and we are plummeted downward, completely broken and stripped of everything we thought mattered in life, we can survive, and with our relationship to Christ still intact. We can represent and honorably shine for Jesus even in the darkness of suffering. Personal pain can be meaningful. Life can still have purpose. *Think It Not Strange* uncovers some of the depths of these secrets. "Eye has not seen, nor ear heard, nor have entered into the heart of man the things which God has prepared for those who love Him" (1 Corinthians 2:9).

Although First Peter 4:12 reminds us not to be surprised, at times it does seem as though the pain comes out of nowhere, crashing into us on our blind sides. We are startled and confused about what to do next. But, as Christians, this valley of decision offers opportunity. Choices are made while walking, running, or even crawling through pain. They are relevant not only to us personally, but they usually affect those around us as well. We may not have control over our circumstances but we do have control of our response to sufferings, despite their origin, and in spite of our never-ending emotions. Is our focal point fixed on what we ourselves are or are not doing, or can we dispatch our concentration to what the Almighty is doing? Do we draw close to Christ during suffering, or pull away? Do we portray faith or hopelessness? Do we rant and rave and defend our outbursts to loved ones (because we are hurting and they should understand); or do we choose to take thoughts captive, and roll them onto God, before they have a chance to steamroll us or others? Sometimes we may even feel God does not care at all. Our reactions may mimic Jesus' disciples in the midst of the storm. They confronted Jesus with "Teacher, do you not care that we are perishing?" (See Mark 4:38-39) We can experience a peace in the storm (as these followers of Jesus did) that surpasses understanding. The plain truth is that God is even more real than our pain. He is not surprised or taken off guard. As the Supreme Sufferer He is a part of all of our sufferings. He knows, He sees, He hears, He is close by. He delivers.

We will pursue these activities of God as we journey through this book. Much will come straight from gleanings in the Word of God. Explore them! "For whatever things were written before were written for our learning, that we through the patience and comfort of the Scriptures might have hope" (Romans 15:4). Oh, that we could be as fellow-sufferer Job, who said that He treasured the words of God's mouth more than his necessary food (Job 23:12).

I also include snapshots from my own pilgrimage with pain. Since this is not an autobiography I won't include all the details that surround each situation I allude to, but these glances will connect us on our individual paths of pain. Many years ago I was living as a Christian missionary in Russia. My husband and I were united by our hearts' desire to serve Christ cross-culturally. But after falling twice on the ice, incurring severe back injury, I was admitted to the hospital. After major surgery and months of "treatments," I was not healing well. It was finally decided that I needed to pursue further care in the United States. It was a devastating blow to our long-range goals. We thought we had initially counted the cost, but we certainly didn't count on that! The degenerative condition I am left with now, after many successive surgeries, has left me in chronic pain. The ministry of prayer and the study of God's Word have sustained me through these many years.

The importance of communicating with the One who can make a real difference in our life of pain cannot be overemphasized. Each chapter ends, therefore, with a springboard prayer for responsive meditation. The lines that follow these prayers are for your own reflections. Pour out your heart to the Lord on this space. Jump into the intimate place of prayerful ponderings, where the Lord will meet you and commune with you by His Spirit. Our souls can be quieted (Psalm 131:2). It may surprise you that aside from a supernatural healing miracle (isn't relief what anyone in pain is searching for?) there are many other forms of healing that you can experience during this difficult time. While you are reading *Think It Not Strange*, look for these treasures under the rubble of your own sufferings. "Now to Him who is able to do exceedingly abundantly above all that we ask or think, according to the power that works in us" (Ephesians 3:20)

CHAPTER ONE

"Why Me?"

"Why is my pain perpetual and my wound
incurable, which refuses to be healed?
Will you surely be to me like an unreliable
stream, as waters that fail?"
(Jeremiah 15:18)

Quiet snowflakes, drifting gently to earth, found their way to my freezing face. Through stiffening, glistening eyelashes I squinted heavenward to look for peace amidst all the commotion. I could not help but look upward. Medical personnel had strapped me to a gurney and were about to load me into an awaiting ambulance. They didn't speak my language, so when I began to cry for God's help I'm quite sure they didn't know I was addressing the only one who really knew what was going on. Desperate for answers, my heart began its interrogation. I still remember the gist of my prayer as the doors slammed me in: "Oh God, why did **this** have to happen **now**?"

I had waited so many years to be a missionary. My husband and I, with our precious four year old son in tow, were serving the Lord in Russia. It was our hearts' desires being fulfilled. God saw me slipping on the ice. He could have protected me from the fall. Why did He allow such a painful injury? Why did He allow me to come to this beautiful country if I were going to end up hurt and unable to do what I thought He had called me to do?

We had so many hopes and dreams. With every cruel stroke that crossed them, one by one, off our life's list, my husband and I asked "why?" In reflecting on that time in my life, I realize that my questions were natural under the circumstances. We are human. People suffer and demand to know the reason. Job did. He asked that question about fifteen times in his book. In the Psalms we can hear hurting ones releasing the question "why?" from the depths of their beings, over and over again. Even Jesus cried out with a loud voice on the cruel cross, "My God, My God, why have you forsaken me?" (Mark 15:34-35). Sometimes it becomes apparent why a season of suffering arrives. Oftentimes, though, we must search the soul, and seek God for the answers. Still, we may never know.

Cloistered in a cloud of confusion, our thoughts spin round and round. Caught in the midst of the pain and heartache are doubts about God's goodness. Even Christians tremble to trust that God is doing the right thing. Sure, we are aware of our contention with the world, the flesh, and the devil. They are relentless in their assault tactics. We can admit there are even those occasions whereby we contribute to our own suffering by making careless, negligent, lazy, compromising or disobedient choices. ("O God, You know my foolishness; And my sins are not hidden from You" ~Ps 69:5).Our hearts are deceitful, we know that. And of course, as a people, we hurt each other. But all these things considered, how do we reconcile the affliction that attacks the seemingly innocent victim? Why would the Lord allow the one seeking Him and set on doing what He wants, to slide into a sea of pain and suffering? Are we able to accept God's goals when they destroy our plans, hopes, and dreams? How? Do we only love Him when what He gives us meets with our approval? Do we believe that He will never leave or forsake us? Can we count on His words in Isaiah 43:2: "When you pass through the waters, I will be with you; and through the rivers, they shall not overflow you. When you walk through the fire, you shall not be burned, nor shall the flame scorch you"?

While undergoing months of testing and treatments in the hospital in Russia, I rapaciously read from the Bible. The word of God was medicinal. It was a lifeline to me; the bridge between reality and insanity. I paused with the mighty man of valor, Gideon, who asked the Angel of the Lord: "… if the LORD is with us, why then has all this happened to us? And where are all His miracles which our fathers told us about" (Judges 6:13). I, too, wanted a miracle! His super power could certainly reach down and touch me for a miraculous healing that would allow my discharge from the hospital and a release to return to my work. So, why hadn't He?

Why had God allowed all this to happen in the first place? I wearied myself thinking these incessant thoughts,and realized I needed to bring my heart's ponderings to the One who knows all things. After all, in Christ are "hidden all the treasures of wisdom and knowledge" (Colossians 2:3).

Like so many inquirers before me, though, I have yet to receive a definitive answer to my question. But that did not make the inquiry insignificant. It was actually in this investment of time that I profited. I was communicating with the Lord, seeking Him, and just as He promises, I found Him to be faithful. In Jeremiah 33:3, the Lord challenges us "Call to Me, and I will answer you, and show you great and mighty things, which you do not know." After I had delved into the research to a depth that had me digging well beneath the layers of my own suffering, I found reconciliation. I was moved beyond the question "why?" and came to realize there can be sufficient compromise within the realm of not knowing. Once I got around the roadblock of my own preoccupation with trying to find the answer to this distracting question, I had a "vision." I saw like I had never seen before. A hand was purposely extended to me, reaching out to give to me. In Job 2:10 I had read "shall we indeed accept good from God, and shall we not accept adversity?" It is absolutely a matter of acceptance. Not just that I allow what comes to me, but that I recognize it as being from God. As I looked past what was in His hand to whose hand it was in, something was settled. But would I ever be able to say, with sincerity, "Even so, Father, for so it seemed good in Your sight" (Matthew 11:26) or echo Job's "though He slay me, yet will I trust Him."?

Remember this chapter's title scripture? "Why is my pain perpetual and my wound incurable, which refuses to be healed? Will you surely be to me like an unreliable stream, as waters that fail?" The answer to this rhetorical question is, "Of course not!" God has been proven reliable. He is trustworthy. These years of study in His Word have left me with an unshaken assurance in that faithful fact. So, if the hand that is giving to me is attached to the entirely honorable Provider, then I should be able to trust Him and accept whatever comes from Him. He is not like Lucy holding the football for Charlie Brown. God is not a tease! He is the Lover of my soul, and yours. We need not be suspicious of the Lord's dealings with us. "Trust in the LORD with all your heart, and lean not on your own understanding." (Proverbs 3:5)

"Can you search out the deep things of God? Can you find out the limits of the Almighty" (Job 11:7)? I don't think we can. That is part of His mystery. The Lord Himself reminds us "For My thoughts are not your thoughts, Nor are your ways My ways," says the LORD. "For as the heavens are higher than the earth, So are My ways higher than your ways, And My thoughts than your thoughts" (Isaiah 55:8-9). We can sigh with the writer of Romans "Oh, the depth of the riches both of the wisdom and knowledge of God! How unsearchable are His judgments and His ways past finding out!" (Romans 11:33) Ironically, though, God does reveal what we *need* to know. Christians have the Holy Spirit Who teaches and guides us into the truth (see John 14:26; 16:13). Sometimes, however, it is frustrating to us for answers to be given on that need- to-know basis. So we must be able to acknowledge the fact that God knows the answer to the question "why?" It is in His safe-keeping. He has a plan and a purpose, which are on a higher plane than we can reach sometimes. God once told a group of people: "I have done nothing without cause that I have done" (Ezekiel 14:23). Do you believe it?

Other biblical writings reiterate that His will is "good, acceptable, and perfect" (see Romans 12:2). Can you rely on it? Agree now, by faith, that He has your times in His hand and all will be arranged for His glory and your good. There must be a settled assurance in one's heart that the Giver is not intending harm to the recipient. The enemy of your soul may use pain to whisper contrary criticisms. If you don't whole-heartedly believe that your heavenly Father wants what's best for you, I beg you to pray on this! Explore the possibility until you own it. Don't cease asking the Lord to work it into your very being. He will. Be encouraged by Jeremiah 29:11: "For I know the thoughts that I think toward you, says the LORD, thoughts of peace and not of evil, to give you a future and a hope." He "works **all things** according to the counsel of His will" (Ephesians 1:11).

Though not always recognizable, there are definitely higher purposes associated with our sufferings and His will. God's Word shows us a chain reaction: "Tribulation produces perseverance, and perseverance, character; and character, hope" (Romans 5:3-4). We cannot expedite trials or tribulations. Suffering saunters, though we try to pull it forward. Sometimes, though, we are compelled to learn patience at its grueling pace. Through this process, though, we are building character. It happens as we seek the Lord and press on in our Christian life. We look to Him for the strength, for the purpose, for the meaning to go on. At the journey's end, the tumult ironically releases hope in our hearts, *"If we can survive <u>this</u>...then what else is possible?"* These are viable spiritual blessings. We can enjoy their benefits if we are open and honest about our need for them.

Jesus suffered and knows best how to comfort the one who is suffering. In our affliction He is afflicted. It is because He has been touched with the feeling of our infirmity that He is able to help. He suffered for us and is able to minister to us because of that bond. He has unlimited resources that come from the pool of who He is and what He has endured. He knows even our soul in adversities and has mercy and grace to extend to us (Psalm 31:7,

Hebrews 4:14-16). The Apostle Paul, too, was such a unique witness of allowing his affliction to be used for something greater in his life. In 2 Corinthians 12:7-10 he wrote: "And lest I should be exalted above measure by the abundance of the revelations, a thorn in the flesh was given to me, a messenger of Satan to buffet me, lest I be exalted above measure. Concerning this thing I pleaded with the Lord three times that it might depart from me. And He said to me, 'My grace is sufficient for you, for My strength is made perfect in weakness.' Therefore most gladly I will rather boast in my infirmities, that the power of Christ may rest upon me. Therefore I take pleasure in infirmities, in reproaches, in needs, in persecutions, in distresses, for Christ's sake. For when I am weak, then I am strong." This was a powerful testimony of the impact of acceptance and submission to God's will for this man's life, despite the hardships. The grace and power that solidified his existence must have had an influence on everyone who came in contact with him (including those who read his words today). He is what is referred to as a "wounded healer." Second Corinthians 1:3-4 illustrates this opportunity for us best:

"Blessed be the God and Father of our Lord Jesus Christ, the Father of mercies and God of all comfort, who comforts us in all our tribulation, that we may be able to comfort those who are in any trouble, with the comfort with which we ourselves are comforted by God." We, too, can be wounded healers just by looking beyond our own discomfort and seizing opportunities to reach out to others. Pray for the Lord to open the way for you to do just that!

A prayer:

Oh, God, why are You allowing this pain? From the depth of my soul I find myself asking this numbing question over and over. You could have intervened, but didn't. You could have prevented this, but chose not to. Why? Lord God, I need You. My heart cries out for the living God. You are the One who can speak peace to the storms. Please help me to sense Your presence, to trust in your abilities, and to be guided by Your Holy Spirit. This life seems too much for me sometimes. I often want to give up, to blame others, including You. See when I am growing dank and bitter, and do something! Crash my perpet-

ual pity parties and take over as guest of honor. Too often I cast shadows rather than reflect light when I suffer. Encourage my heart when I am pleasing You. Be gentle with me, but do what it takes to show me what I may be missing. Surprise me, Lord. Give me "good news, beauty for ashes, the oil of joy for mourning, and the garment of praise for the spirit of heaviness." Help me not to be paralyzed by questions, but to move toward others in need. I long for Your grace, Your mercy, and the assurance that You know what you are doing. I choose, now, to look past what is in your hand, Lord, to Who You are. Teach me more about Yourself. Fill me full with an unshakeable faith. Instill within me the confidence to trust You in the not knowing...why.

_____

_____

_____

_____

_____

_____

_____

_____

CHAPTER TWO

How Long?

❦

> "So I have been allotted months of futility,
> And wearisome nights have been
> appointed to me.
> When I lie down, I say, 'When shall I arise,
> And the night be ended?'
> For I have had my fill of tossing till dawn."
> (Job 7:3-4)

Dear suffering one, have you been thinking your fiery trial will never end? Do you cry out "Have mercy on me, O LORD, for I am weak; O LORD, heal me, for my bones are troubled. My soul also is greatly troubled; But You, O LORD—how long?" (Psalm 6:2-3)? Chains of seconds link to minutes that drag the day by. Weeks soon become months, maybe even years, and yet it seems time has not moved an inch. Is life going on without you because you are stuck in pain's time warp? Are you weary? Does it seem to go on and on even though you are crying and praying—even begging God? Are you feeling like you have waited quite long enough? Do you wonder what God is trying to prove by prolonging your situation?

I have struggled with similar dead-end thoughts through more than twelve years of physical infirmity. Countless cycles of recovery have often left me counting down my very existence on this earth. I have wondered what in the world God was doing and how **He** was passing the time. Was He moving in my midst even though I could not perceive it? In my own long haul with these issues I have learned some things that have helped pass the time. It began when I saw that my clock needed repair.

During one unique season of suffering I was tempted to give up and give in. After years on different pain medications, my doctors decided to try morphine skin patches in preparation for the possible installation of a morphine pump implant. Six months after this progressive experiment the levels in my body became toxic. Later, I was thrown into drug withdrawals. I chose to go through this process at home, rather than in the hospital, though it could have been dangerous had I not had support. Even so, my days went something like this: I was just too tired to sleep. My head was aching and my mind was reeling. My eyes burned and were swollen from constant crying. I was an emotional wreck and my heart felt like it was tearing in two. Sweat poured from my body and yet I was cold and trembling. Nausea was my constant companion. I felt car sick in the house. My skin felt itchy and prickly. I would rock back and forth like a metronome, and yet sound escaped me. I could not focus. Each day brought even more physical pain because the meds were leaving my system. I was constantly checking the clock and the calendar. The doctors had given me a time frame for the severity of the symptoms to ease, and I was holding them to it!

My prayer journal scribbling illustrates my desperation. *"How long, O Lord? Will this ever end? Will it become worse before it gets better? Oh God! I fear I can't bear another minute and still time marches on. Can't You make it stop? Once in Your Word I read that the sun stood still, and the moon stopped, for about a whole day. So surely You are capable, Lord, of just the opposite. How long till the withdrawing is final? How long till the morphine is completely out of my system? What if I can't wait? It seems I am hanging on by only a thread. You see me here, God. How long before this situation changes? In giant print I am writing to remind You that You are the only One who can do anything about this! I just want to die. Help me NOW, Father, oh, please help me now!"*

One thing that kept me sane during this time was reading God's word and listening to praise music to renew my mind. Hour after hour I tried to focus my thoughts on the Lord. He showed me two verses in the book of Isaiah that helped me see that He was, indeed, working on my behalf. The first one was: "Therefore the LORD will wait, **that He may be gracious to you**; and therefore He will be exalted, that He may have mercy on you. For the LORD is a God of justice; blessed are all those who wait for Him" (30:18). His waiting to move out in your situation does not mean the Lord is "kicking back" like we often do during times of inaction. The Lord does not sleep or slumber. He is not slack or lazy. He never wastes time. His timing is perfect. The second verse that brought me comfort was: "For since the beginning of the world men have not heard nor perceived by the ear, nor has the eye seen any God besides You, **Who acts for the one who waits for Him**" (64:4). He has a time for everything and we need only have the sense that God's timing is perfect. Trusting him when we are hurting is an act of faith. Seeing our situation from a timeless perspective requires prayer. There is a miracle, recounted for us in 2 Kings, chapter six, that may help. Elisha prayed for his fearful servant, that God would open his eyes to the unseen. The invisible army was made visible. Those that would be with them were more in number than those on the enemy's side! Greater, too, is Christ in you than anything this life can throw your way.

As long as we are mesmerized by our dark and confusing circumstances, we will be unable to look past ourselves to what's really happening in the spiritual realm (remember, for our good and for His glory). The writer of Ecclesiastes penned: "He who observes the wind will not sow, and he who regards the clouds will not reap" (11:4). We must be still and wait on the Lord! It is not waiting in vain. The important thing is to regard **Who** (not **what**) we are waiting on! We are rendered fruitless when we fix our eyes on our surroundings. Instead, let us take the advice in Hebrews 12:2-3, and "look unto Jesus, the author and finisher of our faith who for the joy that was set before Him endured the cross, despising the shame, and has sat down at the right hand of the throne of God". We must "consider Him who endured such hostility from sinners against Himself, lest you become weary and discouraged in your souls." Psalm 123:1-2 eloquently reiterates: "Unto You I lift up my eyes, O You who dwell in the heavens. Behold, as the eyes of servants look to the hand of their masters, as the eyes of a maid to the hand of her mistress, so our eyes look to the LORD our God, Until He has mercy on us."

We may not see or feel it right away, but God's Word clearly indicates that He is worth the wait. You may be asking, "But just how long do I have to wait?" Two verses in the book of First Peter explain:

"In this you greatly rejoice, though now for **a little while**, if need be, you have been grieved by various trials, that the genuineness of your faith, being much more precious than gold that perishes, though it is tested by fire, may be found to praise, honor, and glory at the revelation of Jesus Christ" (1:6-7). In chapter five, verse ten (of this same book), it says: "May the God of all grace, who called us to His eternal glory by Christ Jesus, after you have **suffered a while**, perfect, establish, strengthen, and settle you." Now I don't know about you, but I want to know what is meant by **a while**! How long was that? When would I know my while was over? In the book of James it says: "Indeed we count them blessed who endure. You have heard of the perseverance of Job and seen the **end intended** by the Lord, that the Lord is very compassionate and merciful" (5:11). What if Job had given up? He surely wouldn't have seen the final blessing, which included "twice as much as he had before." The Bible is clear that: "To everything there is a season, a time for every purpose under heaven" (Ecclesiastes 3:1). The Lord knows when enough is enough. He sees the end of our frayed rope. He does not allow us to go beyond what we're able to endure. He gives strength for the trudging, though only day by day (See Deuteronomy 33:25, Psalm 84:7). The end may not be in sight now, but it does exist. We may not be able to see it while we are prisoners of pain, but there is a release date. "Blessed is the man whom You instruct, O LORD, And teach out of Your law, that You may give him rest **from the days of adversity…**" (Psalm 94:12-13).

Even those dealing with chronic pain can experience closure if they look for it. Think of your life of pain as a book. We know that the last chapter for the believer is in Revelation 21:4. "And God will wipe away every tear from their eyes; there shall be no more death, nor sorrow, nor crying. There shall be no more pain, for the former things have passed away." But what about all the preceding chapters? Are there not small miracle situations in your Christian walk that you can recount? Has God not worked in and through you, time after time? Have you learned anything? Have you reached mini-goals? Have you been transformed emotionally, mentally, or spiritually for good? Have others gleaned from your experiences? Have you inspired someone to have the courage to go on in their journey? Let us look at the completed chapters rather than the unfinished manuscript. Count these blessings! (Let us begin now. Make a list of everything you have to be thankful for. It is a productive distraction and will instill a basis for praise to God. Try it. Stop now and begin a gratitude adventure. It can change your whole outlook.)

Sometimes we have only a full healing in mind. We do not want to consider anything that has to do with learning to live with pain, let alone making peace with it! This is the "all or nothing" blind we pull that keeps us from seeing past our own pitiful situation. We limit exposure to what we deem acceptable. We want what we want and nothing less will do. Sound familiar? Maybe it is time for change in this one area.

Paul wrote to fellow believers "Therefore we do not lose heart. Even though our outward man is perishing, yet the inward man is being renewed day by day. For our light affliction, which is but for a moment, is working for us a far more exceeding and eternal weight of glory, while we do not look at the things which are seen, but at the things which are not seen. For the things which are seen are temporary, but the things which are not seen are eternal" (2 Corinthians 4:16-18). Well, I will have to admit that when I read these verses I was a bit offended. I did not feel very inwardly renewed! And what did the writer mean by light affliction? The Holy Spirit was gentle to remind me, however, that the man who called his affliction "light" also revealed exactly what his afflictions consisted of: "Three times I was beaten with rods; once I was stoned; three times I was ship-wrecked; a night and a day I have been in the deep; in journeys often, in perils of waters, in perils of robbers, in perils of my own countrymen, in perils of the Gentiles, in perils in the city, in perils in the wilderness, in perils in the sea, in perils among false brethren; in weariness and toil, in sleeplessness often, in hunger and thirst, in fastings often, in cold and nakedness, besides the other things, what comes upon me daily: my deep concern for all the churches" (2 Corinthians 11:25-29). If **that** is light, surely mine is even lighter! It is always in the way we look at things. Surely if he could have this perspective, I could. He was human just like I am, and God is no respecter of persons.

Let us remember that God will keep us in perfect

peace if our mind is on Him (Isaiah 26:3). "A bruised reed He will not break, and smoking flax He will not quench" (from Isaiah 42:3). Read that verse again. God is not cruel. "For He knows our frame; He remembers that we are dust (Psalm 103:14). Hang on—the Lord is interceding on your behalf. He is pulling for you! We can be changed even if our pain level remains the same. Job waited on the Lord and believed. "If a man dies, shall he live again? All the days of my hard service I will wait, Till my change comes" (Job 14:14). God will not give up on you. Read the Bible and see all the times it is recounted for us that He is worth our time. Remember: "Jesus Christ is the same yesterday, today, and forever" (Hebrews 13:8). He does not change. You can count on Him. He will not give up on you, so don't you give up either! Jesus emerged from His wilderness experience "in the power of the Spirit" (Luke 4:14), and you can too.

Meditate on the following Psalm references as *you* wait on the Lord:

- Psalm 130:5 - I wait for the LORD, my soul waits,

And in His word I do hope.

- Psalm 57:1 - Be merciful to me, O God, be merciful to me! For my soul trusts in You; And in the shadow of Your wings I will make my refuge, Until these calamities have passed by.

- Psalm 71:20-21 - You, who have shown me great and severe troubles, Shall revive me again, And bring me up again from the depths of the earth. You shall increase my greatness, And comfort me on every side.

- Psalm 27:14 - Wait on the LORD; Be of good courage, And He shall strengthen your heart; Wait, I say, on the LORD!

- Psalm 40:1-2 - I waited patiently for the LORD; And He inclined to me, And heard my cry. He also brought me up out of a horrible pit, Out of the miry clay, And set my feet upon a rock, And established my steps.

A prayer:

Oh, Jesus, help me wait on You! Redeem this time. Give me perseverance and purpose. May I see the eternal view and not look at current circumstances. Help me to focus on You, looking up instead of on things around me. Be the lifter of my head. I don't want to give up on You and try to work things out according to my own limited understanding of the situation. I believe You have the greater good in mind. Help me trust You are working while I wait. Increase my faith, Lord, to endure in Your grace and power. Encourage my heart to not give up. Show me creative ways to pass the time. Help me count my blessings. Keep me prayerful.

_____

_____

_____

_____

_____

_____

_____

_____

CHAPTER THREE

Don't Fall for That!

⸎

> "I would have lost heart, unless I had
> believed that I would see the goodness of the
> LORD in the land of the living."
> (Psalm 27:13)

One of Satan's deceptive lies is well rehearsed during times of suffering. Since the fall of man in Genesis Three, the enemy of our soul has seen its successful results over and over. The well-worn lie is that God is withholding good from us; that we are missing out or that He is holding out. Ultimately, we become convinced that we must, on our own, fill in the "blanks." We believe, as the

Israelites did while waiting for Moses to come off the mountain with the Ten Commandments, that He is taking way too long handing over the goods. (Open your Bible and read about it in Exodus 32.) Instead of taking these thoughts into captivity because they exalt themselves against the true knowledge of God (2 Corinthians 10:5), we mull them over until they make sense to us. We end up, as they did, fashioning our own god to do the job. Eventually we experience bitter regret over our impatience and doubts about God's goodness. If only we will hide Matthew 7:11 in our hearts that we might not sin against Him in this: "If you then, being evil, know how to give good gifts to your children, how much more will your Father who is in heaven give good things to those who ask Him!" Lamentations 3:25 buoys us with "The LORD is good to those who wait for Him, to the soul who seeks Him."

How often have we heard the words "But how can a good God…"? (You fill in the rest of the question.) Perhaps you, like me, have heard yourself murmur it. (It is a cohort of the question, "why me?"). "How can a good God allow all this pain into my life?" What would it take to make this good God better? Is it even possible, or is He just good enough? Consider a few more questions: Would God be altogether good if He did not punish sin and allowed us to do what we want with our lives? Would God be a good God if He could not see our secret sins? Would He be a good God if He did not humble the prideful? Would He be a good God, or any better of a God, if He did not allow any suffering at all? Would He be a good God if He kept to our schedule rather than the unseen realm we can not regulate? Is He only good when He is giving us what we want? Is God only good when we feel good ourselves? In sharp contrast, do we question Him when He pours love, grace, mercy, forgiveness, or blessings into our lives? Questions sure help us take a larger look at our patterns of thinking, do they not? The fact is, that God is good because goodness is a part of His unchanging character. It is not tainted by circumstance or influenced by time. He is not like us! God has rebuked that line of thinking (See Psalm 50:21). He is nothing like us! God is good—always!

The "How can a good God" question is akin to proclaiming, "This just ain't fair!" Well, did you know that **fair** does not always mean **equal**? Do you remember the parable of the vineyard workers? I will not quote the whole passage here. (You can read it in Matthew 20.) The owner of the vineyard hires workers, each at an agreed wage, though at different intervals of the day. When it was time to be paid they all ended up with the same wage. There are angry complaints about this supposed injustice. The boss responds "Is it not lawful for me to do what I wish with my own things? **Or is your eye evil because I am good?**" (Matthew 20:15) We often fall into this trap when we compare ourselves with others. We are warned of this trap in the Word; that it is not wise to measure ourselves by ourselves or compare ourselves among ourselves (2 Corinthians 10:12). God deals with us individually.

What about the story of Joseph, the account of which is written in the final chapters of the book of Genesis? He certainly had reason to cry foul, and yet He was made fruitful in the land of his affliction and even made to forget some of the toil of his father's house (See Genesis 41:50-52; 50:20). Read the whole tale, as it is well worth your time to see all the "unfair" things that happened to Joseph, though ironically, God was with him and continued to show him favor. His example is one reason not to brush off too quickly that often quoted verse in Romans 8:28: "And we know that in all things God works **for the good** of those who love him, who have been called according to his purpose."

In order to defeat the lie, "God is not good," we must have truth in our arsenal of weapons. Besides the basic fact that God is good, there is certainty that He has **our** good in mind. The following is not an exhaustive study, but just a peek into God's goodness through the window of His Word. Let us begin by listening to what the Lord says about Himself while speaking with Moses. "Now the LORD descended in the cloud and stood with him there, and proclaimed the name of the LORD. And the LORD passed before him and proclaimed, 'The LORD, the LORD God, merciful and gracious, longsuffering, and **abounding in goodness** and truth'" (Exodus 34:5-7).

Many times in the book of Deuteronomy we read about obedience as being for the good of the people being instructed. (Oh, how parents wish their children would understand that concept!) For example, it is documented for us that God's intention in the humiliation of the Israelites and their other difficulties while wandering in the wilderness, was **to do them good in the end** (Deuteronomy 8:16). In the book of Jeremiah, God ministers to a people that were in captivity. He said that He had sent them there "for their own good." He continued: "I will set **My eyes on them for good,** and I will bring them back to this land; I will build them and not pull them down, and I will plant them and not pluck them up. Then I will give them a heart to know Me, that I am the LORD; and they shall be My people, and I will be their God, for they shall return to Me with their whole heart" (Jeremiah 24:5-7). Later in Jeremiah it is written: "And I will make an everlasting covenant with them, that I will not turn away from doing them good; but I will put My fear in their hearts so that they will not depart from Me. **Yes, I will rejoice over them to do them good,** and I will assuredly plant them in this land, with all My heart and with all My soul" (Verses 32:40-41). Take a deep breath and proclaim out loud that, "God loves me and wants what's best for me." Go ahead, it feels good!

Now, let's sample the Psalms for encouragements to support God's attribute of goodness:

- "Oh, how great is your goodness, which You have laid up for those who fear You, which You have prepared for those who trust in You in the presence of the sons of men!" (31:19)
- "The LORD is good to all, and His tender mercies are over all His works." (145:9)
- "For He satisfies the longing soul, and fills the hungry soul with goodness." (107:9)
- "He loves righteousness and justice; the earth is full of the goodness of the LORD." (33:5)
- "For the LORD is good; His mercy is everlasting, and His truth endures to all generations." (100:5)
- "Oh, taste and see that the LORD is good; blessed is the man who trusts in Him!" (34:8)

If these few examples have not convinced you of God's goodness, even his goodness towards us, continue to study until you depend on it! Do not listen to the lie of the enemy of your soul. He is incapable of telling the whole truth. There is no truth in him. He is a liar and the father of lies (see John 8:44-

45). His plan is to steal, kill, and destroy. (See John 10:10.) Do not be deceived, like Eve was, so your minds become corrupted from the simplicity that is in Christ. (See 2 Corinthians 11:3.) Let us declare to God (**out loud, right now**): "You are good, and do good; teach me Your statutes" (Psalm 119:68).

A Prayer:

Oh, my Heavenly Father, how I have listened to the enemy's lies about You long enough! In reviewing my life I see the error of my ways. My actions (or lack of them) have proved that I have believed the lie that says you are withholding good from me. When I align those words with Your Word, though, I see the contrast. I can choose to remind myself of your goodness when doubts about it creep into my mind. Thank You for caring so much about me that You want to do me good. Help me not vainly imagine what my life should look like.It's ultimately Yours anyway, isn't it? I want to graciously accept the goodness as well as the adversity, as Job did. I rejoice that, either way it goes, Your word still says, "those who seek the LORD shall not lack any good thing."

_____

_____

_____

_____

_____

_____

_____

_____

_____

_____

_____

_____

_____

_____

_____

_____

_____

_____

_____

_____

_____

_____

_____

_____

CHAPTER FOUR

Invisible Pain

> **"Who are you to judge another's servant?**
> **To his own master he stands or falls.**
> **Indeed, he will be made to stand, for God is**
> **able to make him stand."**
> **(Romans 14:4)**

"I'm so glad you could come. Thank God you're finally getting some relief!"

"But you don't look sick."

"You look great!"

"You sure are walking well."

"It must be nice to not have to work."

"Why can't you just take something?"

"Why don't you try…?" ("Have you tried *this*?"
"Have you tried *that*?")

"My friend had that but she decided not to let it keep her down."

"I can tell you're feeling better."

"It could be worse."

"At least you're getting a lot of rest."

"I wish I had help with my housework."

"I know what you mean, I'm always tired too."

"You're lucky you're able to sleep in every day."

"But you look so good!"

"You sure can't tell anything's wrong."

"You can't die from just being in pain, can you?"

For a long time I have been hearing comments like these. This is not an exhaustive list, by any means, and yet these quotes represent common responses to invisible pain. When a disability is under cover, it is difficult for the well person to relate. There is no reference point for the senses. They may generalize or stereotype according to some other person's experience with a similar situation; or, someone may base their observations on what they themselves experienced at one time or another. It is quite a step of faith to just believe what the sufferer tells them, without seeing any proof. They want to somehow confirm the complaints, lest they be deceived. Of course, they would never come right out and say that they are thinking any of these things, and may even feel guilty for being suspicious, intolerant, or doubting. Whether they want to or not, fit folks may secretly assume that someone with an unseen affliction, looking fine on the outside, is exaggerating, lazy, unmotivated, a complainer, wants pity, are making excuses or even lying, faking it, "milking it," or any number of other incorrect impressions. They may presume the one ill is able to do things they are not really able to do. They question the validity of the restrictions and limitations by which the person in pain is living.

Yes, it is normal to respond first to what one sees. Even the Bible acknowledges that the Lord looks at the heart, but man, well—we look at the outward appearance. (See 1 Samuel 16:7.) We could all ask ourselves, (even suffering individuals), if we have ever judged someone for parking in a handicap parking spot. Maybe the person emerging from a vehicle looks fine, and so we wonder who they think they are or we think they should be ashamed of themselves. Do we really know what is going on inside that person's body, or why they have a placard in their window? Is it any of our business anyway? We must all learn to "walk by faith and not by sight" (2 Corinthians 5:7).

If the healthy individual eventually accepts the invisible pain as true, he or she may still struggle to know the appropriate response to give. The healthy person may fight against sarcasm: "Is terminal pain as bad as terminal cancer?" Loved ones hope against hope that there is a remedy right around the corner. They just want you back to your old self. They want you well, and look for any sign at all that that is happening. Dynamics within family and friendships change. There may even be stages similar to the grief process (shock, denial, anger, anxiety, bargaining, self-blaming, depression) that take place before finally accepting the fact that things are different, and may remain so!

We who have concealed ailments face some unique challenges, also. We endure chronic pain every single day, week after week and year after year, and on top of that have to process the types of comments that are listed at the first of this chapter. We know that our loved ones have a difficult time understanding us because we **look** all right, but deep down we **need** them to understand our pain. **Or do we?** Without question, on both our good days and bad days, we want validation! We are humiliated and frustrated when who we are is defined by what we do. We often feel forgotten, misunderstood, isolated, guilty, disrespected, and discouraged. **But whose fault is that?** Sometimes we who suffer with an invisible disability feel attacked, as though our character and honesty are being questioned. The able-bodied individual does not know what it takes for us to look fine, the courage it takes to leave our homes, knowing that we will probably encounter an increase in pain because we are up and out. We struggle against jealous feelings, because others are able to do so much more than we are. It is difficult for the thriving individual, who does not encounter pain on a regular basis, to know what it is like. Should we wait for them to recognize all the losses in our lives? Should we assume they will understand that moving forward (however slowly) is drudgery, especially with all we are lugging around to accommodate our pain? How are they supposed to know how alone and isolated we feel, especially on dark, sleepless nights? They do not grasp that what people *may* be thinking about us torments us. How can they identify the affect our physical condition has on our relationships, and that it is heartbreaking for us? Unless *they* have suffered with chronic pain, they will not grasp what it takes to reconfigure one's life after dreams are dashed and lifestyles changed, all without our prior written consent!

Then, there are the awful side effects of pain medication, the exasperating waiting for test results, and the defeat we experience after nearly every doctor's visit. We cannot **make** anyone identify with, or appreciate all the energy it takes to address these issues, especially when the pain itself is draining us! We are not simply seeking sympathy or pity **(or are we?)**; but we would like the compassion, consideration, the listening ear—in short— the support of those who supposedly love and care about us. **Yet whose responsibility is it, really, to provide us with these things?** Are we actually judging others we think are judging us?

Will the hale and hearty ever be able to be all that

the person in pain needs? **No!** It is critical to the one besieged by suffering's bedfellows (people-pleasing and unrealistic expectations) to come to grips with the cold hard facts. Oftentimes, a boomerang effect has taken place and we do not even know it. We infirmed individuals generalize those wanting to help and understand, and we judge **them** for not meeting **our** expectations! How ironic and pathetic! Only God can meet our needs. He is the comforter. He is our hope. Only God is sufficient to handle all our concerns. Only God knows the truth about our current situations. Only He can do anything about them! Go to him when you feel slighted. Turn to the Lord when folks "just don't understand." Be desperate for Him! Only He can grasp what pain is doing to your life. <u>It is the Lord who knows more than anyone what we are going through</u>. Read any of the detailed gospel accounts of Jesus' torture, and you will see how He is able to empathize with your physical afflictions. Furthermore, it is written of our understanding Lord:

- "He was despised and rejected by men, a man of sorrows, and familiar with suffering. Like one from whom men hide their faces He was despised, and we esteemed him not" (Isaiah 53:3).

- "I am poured out like water, and all my bones are out of joint. My heart has turned to wax; it has melted away within me" (Psalm 22:14).

- "He was in the world, and though the world was made through him, the world did not recognize him. He came to that which was his own, but his own did not receive him. (John 1:10-11).

So, He understands.

<u>A Prayer:</u>

Oh, God, I admit my frustration with folks that see me only outwardly. I confess imagined scenarios, and I contrive to justify my anger. I don't really know what others are thinking. Forgive me for wanting to be validated by them instead of You. You are my all and all and that is enough. Help me to be understanding when someone makes a comment that does not reflect the true picture of my health. Give me the perimeters of when to clarify their perceptions and when to just leave it alone. They care about me, no doubt, and just want me to feel better. Open my heart to listen and respond lovingly. Remind me of Your all-sufficiency. You see all that this pain brings to my life. You know what it is all about because of what You have suffered. Help me connect with You and have fellowship with You, even on the basis of our sufferings. Deepen my relationship with You that I will know I have all I need in You.

_____

_____

_____

_____

_____

_____

_____

_____

_____

_____

_____

_____

_____

CHAPTER FIVE

What's the Use?

⌘

> **"What strength do I have,
> that I should hope?
> And what is my end,
> that I should prolong my life?"
> (Job 6:11)**

"Oh, how I want to be free from this pain!" "If only I could do more!" "I am good for nothing like this!" Many times and in many different forms, these longings have been expressed by those in chronic pain. Over and over lumps of clay question the Potter's plan. Romans 7:15 says "For what I am doing, I do not understand. For what I will to do,

that I do not practice; but what I hate, that I do."
Now I know that this Bible verse speaks, in context,
about the struggle over our sinful natures. May God
forgive me if I am taking too much liberty here by
saying that this also illustrates one of the battles of
being bedridden. We chronically ill Christians want
to do so much more in our service to Christ than we
are able to. The enemy of our souls hopes we stag-
nate there, and so he does whatever he can to keep us
bogged down in the slough of "what ifs" and "if
onlys." We feel guilty as sin that we are not **doing**
more. We often wonder if "staying by the stuff" is
enough. (See 1 Samuel 30:24's illustration). We
know that we are "complete in Christ" (Colossians
2:10), but it doesn't seem **as** complete as our able-
bodied associates. So just what does the Lord want
from us? Could there be seasons when less is actually more, and really enough?

I remember, like it was yesterday, the physical
sensation of feeling left out and useless. I was looking out from the balcony window of our flat in
Russia. I could see trudging boots in the snow. The
imprints led like a maze to the three of them. My
husband and our nanny were each holding my son's

mittened hands, lugging him along. ("Was that my coat she was wearing?") They were going to yet another church function that I could not attend. Still recovering from back surgery, I was supposed to stay in bed. It was difficult seeing someone "replace" me. Once, my little boy had even accidentally called her "Mommy" before correcting himself. I know I should not have been so sensitive or jealous, but I felt useless. It was as though I was wasting away under my covers.

I felt left out! For a time my son was not sitting on my lap—he was on someone else's. I wasn't at my husband's side, ministering with him, during our New Believer's Home Bible Study. I was *alone* much of the time. **"What is the use?"** I yelled at the Lord. I felt so like the Psalmist who wrote, "I am forgotten like a dead man, out of mind; I am like a broken vessel." Would I ever be made whole? Would I ever be of use again?

Peeling off the useless label ourselves is a sticky procedure. Aren't we supposed to be productive citizens of our community? Well, what if you can not or only half-way can? What if we are stuck somewhere inbetween, like when a label is too far peeled back to put it back on without the attempted removal being noticed? Do we not experience joy when we are doing what we were meant to do in each of our life roles? Just look at Ecclesiastes 5:18-20: "Here is what I have seen: It is good and fitting for one to eat and drink, and to enjoy the good of all his labor in which he toils under the sun all the days of his life which God gives him; for it is his heritage. As for every man to whom God has given riches and wealth, and given him power to eat of it, to receive his heritage and rejoice in his labor, this is the gift of God. For he will not dwell unduly on the days of his life, because God keeps him busy with the joy of his heart." It is natural to want to work. Scripture states that all work is profitable (Proverbs 14:23). It surely seems as though we are not made for inaction, that the Designer intends us to labor. So, what about when we are not "use-able"? How can I enjoy that sweet sleep that Ecclesiastes 5:12 says the laboring man experiences?

Pain is certainly not rest, as some sturdy folks think. Pain involves hard labor! This toil includes the responsibility that we have to "bear fruit" in our lives, even while bearing pain. Thank God for the vine that really does the work for us, if we allow it. Stop now and read all of John 15. We must remain attached to the source of this vital energy. He creates the "vessel unto honor." Without Christ we can literally do nothing! With Him, nothing He requires is impossible! We can actually "do" this life of pain without complaint (Philippians 2:14), unto the Lord (Colossians 3:23), and in love (1 Corinthians 16:14). These are just a few of the "whatever" scriptures. They apply to you. They apply to me. There are no escape clauses— no excuses.

The fruit that should be evident in our lives (though not fully ripe till we are in Glory ourselves) include: love, joy, peace, patience, kindness, goodness, faithfulness, gentleness, and self-control (Galatians 5:22-23). These are called "fruits **of the Spirit**" for a reason. They can miraculously survive our pain levels and break through our moods, to bless others far more than any manual labor would. But we cannot do it without the Spirit of God! Sure, it is tough, and using our infirmity as an excuse for being in the flesh is convenient, but there are consequences. We become embittered, to say the least, and alienate those around us in the process. We grovel guiltily in prayer, and our focus becomes riveted inward. Instead, we can choose to impart something entirely opposite of our pain to those in our company—those watching for the Lord in our life. Even a dejected appearance and a listless attitude proclaim that you are miserable, without having to say a thing. But what does it benefit? The light of Christ in you is not snuffed out, no matter how you feel. Let it shine! This is a labor of love. It is difficult to walk in the Spirit when you are lying down, but it is not unattainable. We **can** be fruitful in affliction, but **will** we?

Staying "use-full," regardless of any physical condition, must involve connected communication with the One Who Created you. (Remember the Vine?) Make an effort to pray. (Of course that means turning off the television!) It is a tough task for some of us, but it will bear fruit for God's glory. Matthew 6:6 illustrates: "But you, when you pray, go into your room, and when you have shut your door, pray to your Father who is in the secret place; and your Father who sees in secret will reward you openly." I imagine Psalm 91:1 also spoken in hushed tones: "He who dwells in the secret place of the Most High shall abide under the shadow of the Almighty." It is a secret place, indeed. Pour out your heart to Him there. Know that "He shall regard the prayer of the destitute, and shall not despise their prayer" (Psalm 102:17). It is a privilege. There are so many good books on prayer, so I will not elaborate here. I encourage you to discover this discipline, which you absolutely **can** do! Seize this season of incapacitation and explore the possibilities of prayer. It is the most important work. James 5:13 resolves, "Is anyone among you suffering? Let him pray. Is anyone cheerful? Let him sing psalms." Occupy much quiet time with the Lord. There are significant sounds no one else can hear but the one whose ear is turned to God. Settled stillness is immeasurable. Seeking Him first brings all we need to our day. Do you feel you "just can't" because you are dark and dry and withered? Ironically, He is the one to go to because He is both fountain and light. He will redeem any exertion toward this end. Lives will be changed, one of them being your own!

Oh, child of God, your life is "hidden with Christ in God", (Colossians 3:3) right? John, chapter one, says that Christ is in the bosom of the Father. If you are in Christ then where are you? The bosom of our Heavenly Father is the sweetest, gentlest, kindest, most nurturing and satisfying place you can find yourself. You have intrinsic value there! Be enraptured there and lose yourself in the Name above all names! As Christians, we were created in God's image. On that foundational basis alone, we have supreme worth. In Him you live and move and have your being (Acts 17:28). Oh, hurting one, don't you see? There, in that precious place of Christ in us, and we in Him, there is undeniable meaning, purpose, and triumph! You are "accepted in the Beloved" (Ephesians 1:6). This does not come up for review. Your performance (or lack thereof) does not change your position in Christ. There is no ladder to climb! Regardless of situation or circumstance, our lives are assessed according to who we are in Christ. Just being a child of God radiates value through <u>everything</u> in our lives, infusing meaning, even into the painful places. "Come to Me, all you who labor and are heavy laden, and I will give you rest. Take My yoke upon you and learn from Me, for I am gentle and lowly in heart, and you will find rest for your souls. For My yoke is easy and My burden is light."

(Matthew 11:28-30)

Personally, I have learned that I am who I am, in Him. My life roles are relationship based, not performance oriented. I am a wife, a mother, a friend, and a neighbor. These are not determined by my activity level. God's love for me, within these roles, does not teeter on my pain scale. It is constant and keeps me centered. Who I am, not what I do, determines my value. There is more to me than what meets the eye.

A Prayer:

"Hear me when I call, O God of my righteousness! You have relieved me in my distress; Have mercy on me, and hear my prayer." Continue to show me what I am supposed to do in this dark place, and all alone. Help me not to live for myself, but for You, Lord. I don't want to be so self-centered, caring only for my own well-being. Help me to look beyond the end of my bed. Deliver me from the futile thoughts of what once was or what could have been. When the disciples asked you, Lord Jesus, "What shall we do, that we may work the works of God?"

You answered and said to them, "This is the work of God, that you believe in Him whom He sent." In that belief cause me to approach You moment by moment, living in Your very presence that I might be fruitful, pleasing in Your sight, and a blessing to those around me.

_____

_____

_____

_____

_____

_____

_____

_____

_____

_____

_____

_____

_____

_____

_____

_____

_____

CHAPTER SIX

Overwhelmed?

⁂

> "We are hard pressed on every side, yet not crushed; we are perplexed, but not in despair; persecuted, but not forsaken; struck down, but not destroyed."
> (2 Corinthians 4:8-9)

I love Paul's writings in the Bible. He was so honest, so real, about the difficult situations in which he found himself. When the times were appropriate, he was quick to throw in the hope, rather than the towel (like he did with the verse above). He has written down for us how he and his crew "were burdened beyond measure, above strength, so that we despaired even of life." Have you ever felt like that? He goes on afterwards to remind us that God has delivered, is delivering, and will yet deliver (2 Corinthians 1:8-10). Later in the same book, in chapter seven, Paul writes "our bodies had no rest, but we were troubled on every side. Outside were conflicts, inside were fears". Powerful! That is overwhelming. That is stifling. But then, he goes on to use that big word, "Nevertheless." That word is so full of meaning for the overwhelmed individual because it focuses on truth. He reminds us that regardless of his predicament, God comforts the downcast (verse 5-6). There is a story in Second Chronicles, chapter 20, wherein Jehoshaphat was afraid of an army coming against his few of a crew and his prayer included the following, which we can all take to heart when we are overwhelmed by any of life's onslaughts. "O our God….we have no power against this great multitude that is coming against us; nor do we know what to do, but our eyes are upon You."

When a person is struggling beneath chronic pain issues, oftentimes emotions are raw. Bundles of feelings seem to climb up on one another until the individual feels suffocated. Reality becomes blurred and it is hard to focus on the truth. We just want out from under "it." This happened to Elijah. Remember him in the Old Testament book of First Kings? He was a party to so many miracle experiences! He related the revelation of God's glory to a bunch of heathens in a magnificent public display of fire breathing special effects. (Read about this wonderful presentation of God's power in 1 Kings 18). He tasted victory right then and there, when all the people saw what was going on and they fell on their idol-worshipping faces and cried, "The Lord, He is God! The Lord, He is God." Then there was a huge outpouring from a fist sized source to close the already miraculous chapter. Next, a raging woman named Jezebel heard of his great exploits. She threatened him in a hot pursuit and swore that he would be dead by the next day. Overcome by the emotions of these combined encounters (even good exciting events can cause stress), and being, no doubt, dog-tired, he ran for his life! Isolated in the wilderness, I believe this hero became overwhelmed with feelings of anger, fear, uncertainty, and depression—just to name a few. In chapter 19, we read "But he himself went a day's journey into the wilderness, and came and sat down under a broom tree. And he prayed that he might die, and said, 'It is enough! Now, LORD, take my life, for I am no better than my fathers!'" Enough was enough, and enough was too much! But an angel came to him twice and ministered to him. So, he pressed onward. Forty days later, though, we find him in a cave recounting to the Lord his zealous faithfulness as a prophet of God. Then he laments: "I alone am left; and they seek to take my life." Then, with His usual earthshaking style, God passed by and tore into the mountain where Elijah was, and ironically spoke in a "still small voice" that eventually set him aright. Are you also tempted to take your own life? It says in First Corinthians 10:13 that: "No temptation has overtaken you except such as is common to man; but God is faithful, who will not allow you to be tempted beyond what you are able, but with the temptation will also make the way of escape, that you may be able to bear it." God reiterated that Elijah was not alone at all. He was not the only faith-ful one left. He still had a purpose on earth and was strengthened in the Lord to go forth.

As if that story is not enough for you to be able to

relate to, I will share a personal angel incident that gave me what I needed to get over an overwhelming episode of my own. It was a particularly difficult week in my journey with this disease, when God's all sufficient grace glowed to overshadow my pains. I was having severe side affects from a very strong drug for nerve seizures. My emotions raged within me. In addition, I got two serious infections that later landed me in an emergency room. My pain was at an all-time high, I felt crazy, and my skin seemed to be crawling inside itself. I became overwhelmed. Why hadn't God healed me? For 10 years my family and friends have prayed for a healing. What was the Lord's purpose in my suffering? I so wanted to be well. I desired to serve Him more out of my home than within it. Why does it seem to just get worse? The questions were smothering my spirit and I began tuning into Satan's ready answers. His plan is to steal, kill, and destroy. He argues with the truth and exalts himself against our knowledge of God (John 10:10, 2 Corinthians 10:5). The struggle seemed to sap the strength I needed to take my thoughts captive into the obedience of Christ, or so I thought.

Much like Elijah, one evening the mounting

stress left me feeling depressed and wanting to die. That was all I could think about: the ultimate relief! Doesn't Revelation 21:4 say: "And God will wipe away every tear from their eyes: there shall be no more death, nor sorrow, nor crying. There shall be no more pain, for the former things have passed away."? I figured I was ready! I defiantly told my husband: "If God does not take my life tonight, I will!" This path of pain has been a long one for my husband too. He had seen me like this before. He would know how to pray for me. I isolated myself in the bedroom and painfully lowered myself onto my knees myself to pray for freedom. I wanted to be free from pain, free from turmoil, free from life. Time seemed to be dragging and the clouds were darkening. Hopelessness filled my heart. I cried and cried and poured out my heart to God. I was tired...so tired.

It was our son's bedtime and I could hear him entreating my husband for permission to go to sleep in our bed. He knew his Daddy would be staying up late with work he had brought home. Soon after the "yes" was granted, my little boy was contentedly crawling under the covers beside me. Though distracted, I continued praying. While asking God to touch me, a sleepy-sweet voice interrupted me with these exact words: "I don't know what I would do without you, Mommy." Why would my small son say that? It was impossible for him to have heard my comment of defeat I inflicted on my husband earlier. My mind reeled with thoughts of the impact my self-ish desire, if fulfilled, would have on my son. What kind of legacy would I be leaving behind? I was quickly convinced that the Lord put those words on my son's lips for me to realize that God was listening to my pleas, and was indeed reaching out to me. There was a battle fuming in the heavenly realm. Jesus was bearing my burden and gently pulling me close; winning me with His love. I responded to my son with a big hug and told him how special he was to me. I offered praise to God for ministering to me, and not long after we were both asleep. "In the multitude of my anxieties within me, Your comforts delight my soul" (Psalm 94:19).

I awoke at 4:00 a.m.—even before my alarm sounded. My husband was sleeping beside me. I had not even heard him come to bed that night. I could just picture my son's limp arms placed around my husband's neck as he hoisted him up, carrying him to his own bed the previous night. I plodded to the living room with a Bible and devotion book in hand (I had recently received this particular devotional as a belated birthday gift). The day's scheduled readings tore through my heart as I devoured the contents. The day's scriptures were:

- John 18:11 - "Then Jesus said to Peter, 'Put your sword into the sheath. Shall I not drink the cup which My Father has given Me?'"
- Luke 22:41-43 - "And He was withdrawn from them about a stone's throw, and He knelt down and prayed, saying, 'Father, if it is Your will, take this cup away from Me; nevertheless not My will, but Yours, be done. Then an angel appeared to Him from heaven, strengthening Him."

My son was **my** little angel last night.

The morning lit up with hope and renewed mercies. The Lord God was upon me to bind up my brokenness, to proclaim liberty to me, to give me beauty for ashes, the oil of joy for mourning, and the garment of praise for the spirit of heaviness (Isaiah 61:1-3). God had seen my sorrows, tasted my tears, and was now comforting me. His light was my life. I spent a long time in God's Word and was gradually strengthened. I would go on in this grace, and with peace that my Lord's intervening presence was with me, just as He promises:

- Psalm 64:17 - "Unless the Lord had been my help, my soul would soon have settled in silence."

God does deliver the soul from death and keeps feet from falling, that we might walk before Him in the light of the living. (see Psalm 56:13)
I'm glad to be able to plead:

- "Hear my cry, O God; Attend to my prayer. From the end of the earth I will cry to You. When my heart is overwhelmed, lead me to the rock that is higher than I. For You have been a shelter for me, a strong tower from the enemy." (Psalm 61:1-3)

<u>And for you who are feeling overwhelmed right this minute:</u>

- "Now may the God of hope fill you with all joy and peace in believing, that you may abound in hope by the power of the Holy Spirit" (Romans 15:13).

Hope is the key. It is linked to a faith by bonds that can't be broken. It is oftentimes tough to understand just how strong this principle is in dealing with hopelessness. Feeling overwhelmed can seem to strip you of your last breath. So, settle down and really take time to think on the verse that led off this chapter's text: **"We are hard pressed on every side, yet not crushed; we are perplexed, but not in despair; persecuted, but not forsaken; struck down, but not destroyed**. Read it over and over and even imagine the words fitting your situation. Get some dialogues going. For example, "I am feeling pressure from every room of this house right now with all there is to do around me and no energy or ability to do any of it....BUT I am not crushed into this corner and there are some things that have been done and there are some folks that have offered to come over and help me out so I don't feel so compressed. I am perplexed as to what to do about my medications and lately I have been bombarded more by the different opinions I am receiving than even all the different side effects, BUT I am not in despair because there are professional resource materials available to me in the brochures I brought home from the doctor, on the internet, in medical journals and even books friends have loaned me that I never have gotten around to read (not to mention the "wisdom from above"), so I am definitely not at the point of despair yet! And as far as being forsaken, well, wasn't it just this morning that I read about the Holy Spirit being in me and that there is no where I can go from that Helper? Prayer is a breath away and so I am neither struck down nor struck out, am I?" This will help you in the here and now (this moment). In Deuteronomy, Chapter Four, during a distressful time, ("**when all these things come upon you**"), the people responded from the place they found themselves in then. "But **from there** you will seek the Lord your God; and you will find Him if you seek Him with all your heart and with all your soul." This is the same God that knew this peoples' trudging through the great wilderness and yet was with them and they lacked nothing (mentioned just two chapters before this). The Lord doesn't change. He sees us as He saw those loved ones. Remind yourself in prayer *now*, "I will be glad and rejoice in Your mercy, For You have considered my trouble; You have known my soul in adversities" (Psalm 31:7).

Now let's look at the future. Being overwhelmed without sensing hope can be relieved in the long term as well. We rally ourselves for now and for later. (But I do not mean venturing into the realm of "what ifs"!) Stick with the truth and what is real. As long as God is still on the throne and you are not dead yet, there is still hope!

That is why it says in 1 Corinthians 15:19 (emphasis mine) that "**if <u>in this life</u> <u>only</u> we have hope in Christ, we are of all men the most pitiable**". There *is* more than this! The tough thing, though, is that it brings us back to faith and hope, and those are not always tangible, the way we would like. Think through these verses:

- "For we were saved in this hope, but **hope that is seen is not hope**; for why does one still hope for what he sees? But if we hope for what we do not see, we **eagerly wait for it with perseverance"** (in Romans 8:24-25).

• Hebrews 11:1 - "Faith is the very substance of things hoped for; the **evidence of things not seen."**

So, once again, there is faith and there is hope. We hang on to them with all we've got and believe that God's Word is true. One day it will all be worth it. Memorize this promise in Revelation 21:4, and muster up the courage to accept the fact that you will not see it fully realized *this side* of heaven. Nevertheless, it is a blessed hope: "And God will wipe away every tear from their eyes; there shall be no more death, nor sorrow, nor crying. There shall be no more pain, for the former things have passed away."

A Prayer:

Oh, Father in heaven, I want to believe with the Psalmist that "in the multitude of my anxieties within me, Your comforts delight my soul." Lord,

Your Word says "hope does not disappoint". Help me believe it! Come to my rescue and cause me to hope against hope. I know that ultimately You are my refuge and my strength, a very present help in times of trouble. Don't let my heart be troubled. Calm this storm and instill peace in me. Help me trust You. Open the eyes of my understanding, that I might be enlightened, even in my present state, and to know what is the hope of your calling for me. I want to be "rejoicing in hope, patient in tribulation, continuing steadfastly in prayer," but I can't seem to muster up the steam. Equip me to fight the good fight of faith and help me see the light at the end of this tunnel. Thank You for anchoring my soul so that I never have to believe I am falling off the edge. I declare now that I am hard pressed on every side, yet not crushed; I am perplexed, but not in despair; I may be persecuted, but I'm not forsaken; struck down, but I'm not struck out!

_____

_____

_____

_____

_____

CHAPTER SEVEN

Letting Go
⌘

> "Brethren, I do not count myself to have apprehended; but one thing I do, forgetting those things which are behind and reaching forward to those things which are ahead, I press toward the goal for the prize of the upward call of God in Christ Jesus."
> (Philippians 3:13-14)

This chapter was particularly difficult to write. Tears spilled out onto my words, making a blurry mess of what has already been sorted out in my mind. Letting go of a longing stretches the heart to almost bursting, and the tears do eventually leak out, do they not? Like the unpredictable emotions connected to a long-lost love, the charged memories spark without warning. It can take your breath away! I have indeed, let go, and I have made peace with who I am now in my life. Still, though, the sadness sneaks in from time to time to remind me of "what could have been."

I will begin by reading a relatively important excerpt from my prayer journal.

"It was a good goal, wasn't it Lord? "It is for the benefit of others rather than me, right? You could still heal me with one of your miracles, God. You could change our circumstances. You could enable me to serve You again in Russia. But You have not, You are not, and there's no indication that You will. So, Lord, where does that leave me? There's an emptiness that comes with relinquishing my dream. There's a hole that will need to be filled or else I will be incomplete, won't I? What if you replace it with something that isn't as good, or something that doesn't give me the same pleasure? Is the best just gone for good? I feel like

I've been let down, and I might add, not so gently. So, what now?"

Eight years have now passed since that writing. I have explained the basis of this damaged dream in the introduction of this book. I will not echo it here. Suffice it to say that coming "home" from our mission work was one of the hardest things I have had to do in my life. I got off track not long afterward because I was not willing to accept God's will and, instead, clung on to the hope of going back there to live. Actually, I hung on till my knuckles were numb. Hope deferred surely does sicken the heart! (Proverbs 13:12)

Through the years, since our "untimely" return and all the readjustments, I have struggled with "getting over it. "With each prayer for a missionary, and whenever I saw a team leave from our church to go overseas, I would lament my new placement. I cried to friends that God had not taken the love we had for Russia or its people out of our hearts. I secretly hung on to the hope that we would one day return to live there, in spite of my physical condition, and despite what God might be thinking about it. I would not loosen my grip!

Would God have to pry the gift He once gave me out of my clenched fist? I brought my fantasy of returning to Russia to each and every doctor appointment. I took it with me into each of the eight operating rooms I have visited for back surgery. I was obsessed. It was as if it was my right to be well again and back to my work. It was my preoccupation during any ministry conversation. 1 Corinthians 6:12 would later help to wake me up from this state, when I read: "All things are lawful for me, but all things are not helpful. All things are lawful for me, but I will not be brought under the power of any." One friend even commented, "It's as though you don't have a life outside of Russia!" I became inwardly discouraged and disillusioned; miserable minding the store when everyone else was out doing something I thought more significant. I surely was exerting a lot of energy in that rocking chair!

My long-held and deeply cherished dream was shattered! The Lord even allowed me to see myself, in a vision of sorts. Down on my knees, crawling through the broken pieces, bleeding and encrusted with the fragments while still trying to salvage the remnants of what could have been. After many grueling years I was desperately weary and frustrated. Pathetic,huh? But God, indeed, does "raise up all who are bowed down" (Psalm 146:8).

Long ago, God relayed (through Moses) to the children of Israel that they were a stiff-necked people. He said, "I could come up into your midst in one moment and consume you." (Exodus 33:5) I am thankful I never heard the Lord say anything like that to me during my ranting about what was unfair in my life (well, maybe He did but I wasn't listening at the time). I had been stomping my foot, even while on my knees. My stubborn striving with what I thought I "should be," though, eventually did take its toll. Even my vision was blurred when I finally rose out of the rubble. I finally came to understand that I needed to search inside, in stillness, for the perpetrator. Through the chaos and heartache of such ponderings, God Himself, by that precious Holy Spirit of His, led me to an accurate depiction of my condition.

First, I repented of holding a grudge against God for having allowed the injury that instigated our return to the states. I belong to Him. My life is not my own. I gave Him "permission" upon my conversion years ago, to do with me as He wants to. If it pleased the Lord to bruise His own Son (see Isaiah 53:10), why not me, or any of His other children? I had been duped again by the age-old Satanic lie that says "God is holding out on you." Job had it right when he said ... "The LORD gave, and the LORD has taken away; Blessed be the name of the LORD," and "... Shall we indeed accept good from God, and shall we not accept adversity?" (Job 1:21; 2:10) So began the mending process.

The Lord is so patient and has been oh so kind in His workings to woo me back to my first love. Over the years, little by little, my cause has crumbled. He showed me the digression of my relationship with Him and the root of my emotional pain and mental anguish. After letting go of the grudge against God, next was the exposure of idolatry in my life. Idolatry is such an alien word nowadays, but probing further, I would come to understand the reality of its destructive power. I had allowed my desire for Russia to grow stronger than my desire for God. I was caged by what I wanted for my life and was not free to allow Jesus to *be* my life. My hopes, dreams, desires, and goals were subtly and gradually gaining pace to overtake what was Supreme—my relationship with Christ. Where I went wrong can be compared to a principle of flesh versus spirit. These forces are at war within us, right? (See Galatians 5:17, for example.) Well, the one we care for best, nurture, feed, and cater to is the one that will emerge stronger. I had looked after my fantasy relationship with a washed-out wish more ardently than my soul's longing for God. My spirit's craving became muted by the flesh's blubbering. It did not seem as though Jesus would satisfy me in quite the same way my hope would. Maybe I did not think I would derive the same pleasure from Him that I received from my vain imagination. The Lord, my God, had become the mere means to my end. I was involved with the lesser god of good intentions.

I was not prepared to give back, as a love offering, this gift God had given me to enjoy. Remember Hannah in the Old Testament? She worshipped with open arms, palms up: "For this child I prayed, and the LORD has granted me my petition which I asked of Him. Therefore I also have lent him to the LORD; as long as he lives he shall be lent to the LORD. So they worshiped the LORD there" (1 Samuel 1:27-

28). How had my arms gotten so wrapped around myself, and my own interpretation of what "my" life should be? We must take delivery of God's gifts, blessings, talents—even the hopes and dreams in our hearts, ready to release them back to Him if He asks.

Now it is very important here to understand that release does not always mean relinquish. When it does, though, there will be a redirection that is just as meaningful! Remember Abraham and Isaac from Genesis 22? Abraham's thoughts and actions proved his willing intention to offer up what was precious to him in his life. He did not, however, have to ulti- mately give it up. The Angel of the Lord stopped him in his tracks and said, "Now I know that you fear God, since you have not withheld your son, your only son, from Me." In contrast, chapter 16 of the book of Acts tells a different story. It tells us that the churches were strengthened in the faith, and increased in number daily. This was in large part due to the Apostle Paul's travels. Yet in verses six and seven, it tells us that he and Silas were forbidden by the Holy Spirit to preach the Word in Asia. Then, they tried to go into Bithynia, but the Spirit did not permit them to go there either! This turned out to be by divine guidance and direction. And yet, right after these verses we are shown that a vision appeared to Paul in the night. A man of Macedonia stood and pleaded with him, saying, "Come over to Macedonia and help us." Now after he had seen the vision, immediately they went there—"concluding that the Lord had called us to preach the gospel to them" (verses 9-10). Both of these stories illustrate the importance of walking flexibly by faith. Being bendable enough to conform to God's plan of action.

Now I will get back to my testimony. First, I confessed the grudge against God, then I was shown I was worshipping a lesser god, and Psalm 16:4 was right in predicting that my sorrows would be multiplied as I hastened after another god. *But* I thank the Lord that idolatry is a sin! There is a remedy for that! The precious blood of Jesus covers sin, (not excuses, not defenses, not explanations, not exemptions, but sin!). I confessed and have since repented, and as expected, God was "faithful and just to forgive" me my sins and to cleanse me from all unrighteousness (1 John 1:9). My attention is redirected. God again became my gold and my precious silver; then I delighted in the Almighty (Job 22:25-

26). I was finally at peace like the illustration in Psalm 131: "I have calmed and quieted my soul, like a weaned child is my soul within me."

Now I can pray more effectively for Russia. It seems I have an even greater missions burden in my heart than before, though now I am a sender and supporter rather than a "goer." I am not clogged anymore with my own expectations of what my life should look like. Psalms 62:5 admonishes me: "My soul, wait silently for God alone, For my expectation is from Him." And Psalm 39:7 says: "...now, Lord, what do I wait for? My hope is in You."

So, even after eight spinal operations (and at this writing another one around the corner) my mission is still to be about my "Father's business." For me that includes being a daughter of God, a wife, mother, friend, and neighbor. The Lord has shown me how to be faithful to Him within each of these roles; satisfied with His sufficiency for me. "Not that we are sufficient of ourselves to think of anything as being from ourselves, but our sufficiency is from God" (2 Corinthians 3:5).

How about you? Are you spinning your wheels, like I was for so many years, but going nowhere?

Maybe you are not meant to be going or doing where you think. Maybe this enforced idleness is for a reason. Do not miss the opportunity to free your spirit from your imprisoned body! Move in your God-given roles, using the gifts He gives you. What if God told you to start crossing things off your to-do list? Would you obey Him? What if not looking beyond where you are this instant, content being His, is the "one thing" He is asking of you at this point in your journey with Him? Would that be do-able? (Do not go away sad like the rich young ruler in Luke, chapter eighteen, who could not do the "one thing" Jesus asked of him.) Stop now and ask the Lord what you should or should not be pursuing. There are so many possibilities, unique to your physical situation. Let me ask you a hard question from Jeremiah 45:5: "Do you seek great things for yourself?" Feelings of being constricted and restricted overshadow the "small things" sometimes. What ever happened to simplicity and contentment? Naaman was a mighty man of valor in the Old Testament. He was honorable. He was a leper. Leprosy was an incurable, isolating, ulcerous, flesh-rotting disease. In brief, Naaman's leprosy *was* curable, and he was advised just how he could be healed. (You can read the full story in 2 Kings, chapter five.) The suggested remedy, though, angered him. He wanted a more spectacular solution from the Lord. Perhaps his pride was standing in the way of God's will? His servants confronted him with the question that if he had been told to "do some great thing," wouldn't he have done it? "How much more," they continued, should he follow the simple instructions he was given. Eventually, he did. When Naaman moved out of the way he was healed of leprosy. (I certainly don't mean to imply here that our obedience to whatever God calls us to do is the source of our physical healing. Maybe you are not even striving for "great things" for yourself. Perhaps you just want a bit of "normalcy" to return to your life. Is that too much to ask? Letting go, for you, may mean just letting the Lord minister his sweet love to your heart. Keep your hands open and ask for all God has for you. But, for others of you who are dragging your dream along behind you (wondering, like I was, when it was going to hurry and catch up) maybe the time to let go is now—this moment. Release it to God and ask Him to redirect you for His purposes.

In part, 1 Chronicles 28:9 says: "the Lord searches all hearts and understands all the intents of the thoughts." Just as God knew it was in David's heart to build a temple (though he was prevented from doing so), the Lord said to him "whereas it was in your heart, **you did well that it was in your heart**." (See 1 Kings 8:18.) He did not scheme or try to manipulate the situation to do it anyway, because he was a man after God's own heart! Sometimes we just have to forget about the closed doors behind us and move on to the open ones in front of us. (I have learned not try to pry them open). We do not have to see ourselves as shelved when the Lord redirects us. There are other opportunities. Psalm 37:23 says that "the steps of a good man are ordered by the LORD, and He delights in his way." Our lives are ordered **by the Lord**—not by doctors, family, friends, preachers, (though certainly God uses many of these as resources to administer His will), T.V. gurus, or our own mind's eye. God has a plan. Jeremiah 29:11 says it best: "For I know the thoughts that I think toward you, says the LORD, thoughts of peace and not of evil, to give you a future and a hope." I love that He used both the words **future and hope.**

A Prayer:

Lord God, do I need to "let go" of some good thing that is in competition with the better thing of Your having Your rightful place in my heart? Am I too distracted by anyone or anything, or have I been brought under its power? Have any of Your gifts become more important than You, the Giver? Am I holding onto any hope or dream that You want me to sacrificially offer to You? Make Your will matter to me. Am I making excuses or holding back? You know me. You know the thoughts and intents of my heart. I want the future and hope laid out for me before I was even born. Must I let go of anyone or anything? Help my thoughts and actions show I am willing to do as You ask. If the air has to be let out of my balloon let me down gently. Your Word says that you are near to the brokenhearted. Help me sense it. Minister to my disappointment. Thank you for giving me all I need to be content in You. Revive me again and give me vision for what's up ahead as You redirect my path.

CHAPTER EIGHT

Making Peace with the Pain
❦

> **"Why is light given to him who is in misery,
> and life to the bitter of soul?"
> (Job 3:20)**

The answer is that God isn't finished with you and you are not dead yet! You are alive. You may not feel alive, you may not look alive, but science and medicine explain brain activity and breath as life. "The Spirit of God has made me, and the breath of the Almighty gives me life" (Job 33:4). There is a divine reason you and I are here, regardless of our physical state. "You are worthy, O Lord, to receive glory and honor and power; for You created all things, and by Your will they exist and were created" (Revelation 4:11). We are God's "workmanship" (Ephesians 2:10). If we are Christians, we have been "bought with a price" and are not our own anymore (1 Corinthians 6:19-20). We are not to be living for ourselves anyway, but for Him who died for us and rose again (2 Corinthians 5:15). Whew! There are so many of these scriptures to encourage us (even as we have already explored in other chapters of *Think It Not Strange*) that we are of worth! The Lord has a plan and purpose for each of us in this life, in spite of our pain levels. It is vital that we take this to heart.

As long as you and I are not dead yet, we have access to God's divine power! The LORD will strengthen you on your "bed of illness;" and sustain you on your sickbed (Psalm 41:3). Isaiah 40:28-29 asks " Have you not known? Have you not heard? The everlasting God, the LORD, The Creator of the ends of the earth, Neither faints nor is weary. His understanding is unsearchable. He gives power to the weak, And to those who have no might He increases strength." What kind of strength? Is it enough for you? Read on! The Word says that it is the "exceeding greatness of His power" that works toward us who believe in Him, and that it is the same power that worked in Christ when He was raised from the dead (see Ephesians 1:19-20)! God "has given to us all things that pertain to life and godliness, through the knowledge of Him who called us by glory and virtue, by which have been given to us exceedingly great and precious promises..." (2 Peter 1:3-4). Find out what those promises are for your life. Poke around in the Word. Investigate its claims. Probe deeper still. "Eye has not seen, nor ear heard, nor have entered into the heart of man the things which God has prepared for those who love Him" (1 Corinthians 2:9). Ephesians 3:20 heightens the expectation: "Now to Him who is able to do exceedingly abundantly above all that we ask or think, according to the power that works in us, to Him be glory in the church by Christ Jesus to all generations, forever and ever. Amen."

You may be thinking, "Wouldn't it just be easier for Him to heal me?" Or, "Isn't it possible for God to still heal me?" Yes. It is possible. "For with God nothing will be impossible" (Luke 1:37). We belong to a big God with unlimited resources! Making peace with chronic pain includes believing that the good Lord is able to heal you and in the meantime, to minister both **to** you *and* **through** you. It is my conviction, however, that God does not **always** choose to heal his children. (oh, please don't toss this book into the trash can yet, you're on the last chapter!) Perhaps His purposes would be better served within an illness' arena of confinement. I know that a lot of people within the Christian community believe that it is our "right" as children of God, to be healed. Many base their belief on Isaiah 53:5, which says "But He was wounded for our transgressions, He was bruised for our iniquities; the chastisement for our peace was upon Him, and by His stripes we are healed." It is not my intention in this chapter to debate this. I will however, imme- diately address the fact that some have fallen prey to the lie that **all** physical pain comes as a direct result of sin (or lack of faith) in one's life. That is simply not true. The resulting condemnation often leads to guilt-ridden self-absorption. This is detrimental to the sincere soul seeking answers. We can always ask the Lord to search our hearts and reveal sin to us. We have an Advocate with the Father. He is faithful and just to forgive us our sin when we confess it to him (I John 1:9). We repent and move on. It is Satan, though, who is the "Accuser of our brethren" (Revelation 12:10), **but without any remedy**. He wants us to wallow in the depths of despair over our unrighteousness. It is unfruitful; of benefit to nobody but the evil one. Though there are cases where there is a direct correlation to sin, there are many more states of affairs where sin is not the cause. In just one instance I will recount, Jesus' disciples were discussing the condition of a blind man. Jesus then proclaimed, "Neither this man nor his parents sinned, but that the works of God should be revealed in him" (John 9:3). It is plain and simple.

There are many examples in the Bible on which to base hope for a healing. God Himself has told his people "**I am the LORD who heals you**" (Exodus 15:26). It is He "Who forgives all your iniquities; **who heals all your diseases**" (Psalm 103:3). Besides these, there are so many Old and New Testament Scriptures that portray supernatural healings. Do a Bible Study on this topic. There is a plethora of proofs and reasons why we can commit our physical infirmities to Him. We can turn them over to the One who can do something about it if He chooses, "casting all your care upon Him, for He cares for you" (1 Peter 5:7). I will pick just one example from a myriad of healings Jesus performed. Remember Lazarus? His sisters sent to Jesus, saying "Lord, behold, he whom You love is sick" (John 11:3). "When Jesus heard that, He said, "This sickness is not unto death, but for the glory of God, that the Son of God may be glorified through it." He was eventually healed and God did get glory for it. On the other hand, we have an equally loved and chosen-of-God man named Paul. He himself pleaded with the Lord to pluck out the "thorn" in his flesh. God answered that **His grace was sufficient** and that God's strength is made perfect in weakness. (See 2 Corinthians 12:7-10.) No doubt it was not what Paul wanted to hear. He had been a faithful servant. Why not just heal him? Why was the Lord's disciple Timothy told to "no longer drink only water, but use a little wine for your stomach's sake and your frequent infirmities" (1 Timothy 5:23)? Why didn't the Lord just touch his tummy and make it all better? In addition, history reveals that many godly saints and martyrs died not only ill, but suffering. That is life in this old world.

God **can** at all times heal but does not always choose to do so. He has His reasons! Either way, we pray and we ask and yes, we sometimes beg, but always under the umbrella of His will for us. Never give up! Never give in! Pray without ceasing. The "prayer of the upright is His delight" (Proverbs 15:8). "Be anxious for nothing, but in everything by prayer and supplication, with thanksgiving, let your requests be made known to God; **and the peace of God, which surpasses all understanding, will guard your hearts and minds through Christ Jesus** (Philippians 4:6-7).

As I have alluded to several times in *Think It Not Strange*, I believe that healing comes in many varieties. It is a huge blessing to those around you when you receive an attitude adjustment (which oftentimes cures the countenance as well). There are emotional, mental, and psychological healings. Being delivered from a hurtful tongue is as valuable as a full-body healing, as is illustrated by these two scriptures:

- "Death and life are in the power of the tongue" (Proverbs 18:21).

- "Whoever guards his mouth and tongue keeps his soul from troubles" (Proverbs 21:23).

The restoration of joy is a therapeutic procedure.

- "A merry heart does good, like medicine, But a broken spirit dries the bones" (Proverbs 17:22).

It is just as momentous to have your heart healed of sin and doubt as to be cured of a long time illness. Just think of the eternal, unquenchable, fiery, pain that will never touch you, if you are Born Again into life everlasting in Christ. **Now *that* is healing!**

- "Repent therefore and be converted, that your sins may be blotted out, so that times of refreshing may come from the presence of the Lord" (Acts 3:19).

Begin to think of many more "healings" that you have already experienced on your own path of pain.

Rejoice in them. Look for them. Jot them down as to their significance in your walk with the Lord and how they can pleasantly affect others for Him.

Gratitude and praise to God also have restorative properties (are you still counting your blessings or making up a catalog of gratitude?)

Or, quite honestly, is all this just hard to digest? Does it seem too quaint and simplistic? Are you finding it hard to stomach the fact that you may "just have to learn to live with it?" What are you being dispossessed of that is making it difficult for you to make peace with chronic pain? In the final chapter of Habakkuk, the prophet assessed his state of affairs and wrote: "Though the fig tree may not blossom, Nor fruit be on the vines; Though the labor of the olive may fail, And the fields yield no food; Though the flock may be cut off from the fold, And there be no herd in the stalls—**Yet I will rejoice in the LORD, I will joy in the God of my salvation** (Habakkuk 3:17-18). Keep reading and you will be able to understand, though you may be asking (as I did the first time I read this), "so what does vegetation (or the lack thereof) have to do with helping *me* in *my* painful situation?" So, I integrated my life's properties with Habakkuk's theory and finagled the following updated-just-for-me version: (Try it with your own particulars). *"Though I wake up with the same pain I go to sleep with, though I am more often alone than in the company of friends and family, though I wish I were able to do so much more than I'm doing now, though my emotions drain me and my thoughts weary me, though my pain meds complicate things more than providing relief...* **"Yet I will rejoice in the LORD, I will joy in the God of my salvation."** It is a choice. It is a frame of mind that demands that we focus more on the Almighty than on ourselves. Why? Because He is worthy of our praise and adoration-regardless of our crummy circumstances (which, by the way, may not seem so shabby after you begin to praise Him for all His benefits)! What shall I render to the LORD for all His benefits toward me" (Ps 116:12)? Bless the LORD, O my soul, and forget not all His benefits (Psalm 103:2). Will we do as similarly encouraged in James 1:2? "My brethren, count it all joy when you fall into various trials...." **God is worthy of our praise.** We *can* rejoice in who He is, but *will* we? He is all we need for whatever each day brings. His precious thoughts toward us are more than can be numbered. God's eyes saw our substance before it was even formed in the womb. He has fashioned our days and in His book they are all written. Please take time to read and pray back to the Lord Psalm 139. Pray, too, Psalm 90:15 "Make us glad according to the days in which You have afflicted us, The years in which we have seen evil." He can do it! Nothing can separate you from His love (read Romans 8:35-39)! Nothing!

I will close this chapter with several battle cries in the form of my prayer for you. I love to pray scripture back to the Lord since my words seem so trivial in comparison. Stop now and get as "comfortable" as possible and slowly read over my intercession for you. (Though almost all straight from the Bible, but I will not entangle the references among the sentences as I have done throughout much of this book. Look the words up in a concordance to pinpoint their address. Many are already familiar friends to the sufferer in Christ.) **Ask the Lord to help you make peace with your pain and move forward to all He has planned for you as His beloved child.**

Prayer for you:

Lord God, thank you for being the Alpha and the Omega, the Beginning and the End, Who is and Who was and Who is to come, the Almighty! I bow to you on that basis alone, and come humbly before Your throne of grace; to find mercy and grace to help—for not only myself, but all those reading this book right now that hurt. All things were created through You and for You, including we humans. Though it's hard to understand the depth of Your unconditional love for us and though we certainly don't deserve it, I thank you. I appreciate, Lord Jesus, that you became for us wisdom from God and righteousness, and sanctification, and redemption. What would we do without You?

I trust that Your will is good, acceptable, and perfect though sometimes it doesn't make sense to me. So many times I pray the "why me?" prayer and still you shine light into my darkness and into my heart to bring back the simple joy of my salvation. Do that for any of my readers now that need that special touch of warmth, light or a spring of refreshment, where they now sense only cold, hard, damp ground. You are the God of Hope! Wow! Instill it deeply into the suffering seeker. Help their unbelief even if it means doing that fancy thing you do in giving life to the dead and calling those things which do not exist as though they did.

Be their Wonderful Counselor, Mighty God, Everlasting Father, and Prince of Peace. I don't know what they need at this exact moment, but You sure do. Thank you that Your understanding of their condition is dependable and consistent. Give some of that to those doctors making decisions on their behalf. Heal supernaturally, Lord, as we believe you can, and rock the medical community as they encounter Your power! Give sufficient grace for those You choose not to physically heal. Show them how you can remove the cause and affects of so many other aliments too, those often far more serious. (Those not in the medical journals.) Illuminate minds and decontaminate characters. Make attitude adjustments and tweak temperaments. With so many promises of your help, all filthiness of both flesh and spirit can be made right in you. Thank you for that hope for this life and of course for our future change when <u>all things</u> are new, including our bodies!

Halleluiah!

Help those afflicted with chronic pain to not lose heart, that they would reap in due season. Rejoice over them with singing. Surround them with songs of deliverance. May they watch, stand fast in the faith, be brave, and be strong! Assist them to endure hardship as good soldiers of Jesus Christ. Modify the finish time if you must, only keep their pace steady to finish well. Keep us all in Your word of truth, The Bible. Instruct in patience and establish hearts because Your coming is at hand. Thank you for that Blessed Hope!

Satiate all those weary souls and replenish the sorrowful ones. Strengthen spirits that they would know they will have all they need pertaining to life and godliness. Minister Your sweetness to their spirits through loved ones, friends, even strangers-who we know may be your angels. Assure them that you are on guard, on watch, knowing even the deepest desires and quietest secrets of their hearts. Ignite their inner most being by Your Holy Spirit, and fine tune the forming of even a whisper, which would begin prayers of their own. Have them know that You, indeed, hear them. Moment by moment I pray,

Lord, that they would draw near You and as You have promised-be near them. Allow them to sense that they are not alone and that You are indeed love itself. You are real love, complete love; the kind that casts out even fear. Infuse them with the authenticity of Your unmatchable, unchanging, peaceful presence that will never fail nor forsake them. In Jesus' Name I pray, Amen.

_____
_____
_____
_____
_____
_____
_____
_____
_____
_____
_____
_____
_____
_____

Printed in the United States
38863LVS00007B/10-147

9 781591 605492